49 Questions to Annoy Your Parents

Copyright © 2015, 2022 by James Warwood

Published by Curious Squirrel Press

Book cover design by: James Warwood
Book interior design by: Mala Letra / Lic. Sara F. Salomon

ISBN: 9798425835017
ebook ISBN: B00YWL439C

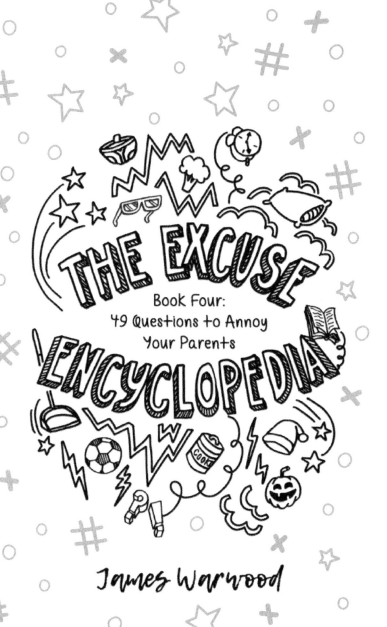

THE EXCUSE

Book Four:
49 Questions to Annoy
Your Parents

ENCYCLOPEDIA

James Warwood

BOOK FOUR

Questions to Annoy Your Parents

ANNOYING QUESTIONS

1. THE SHOES QUESTION

You know when you said *'they've got a tough life, you should try walking in their shoes'* . . .

. . . I'm wearing their shoes now and I've been walking for miles. I still don't understand their hardships, in fact I think I've just made it worse by stealing their shoes.

2. THE VAMPIRE QUESTION

Would a Jewish Vampire cower at the sight of a Christian cross? . . .

. . . because if not I will start carrying around a symbol for every major world religion, just in case I'm attacked by a spiritually curious vampire.

3. THE FRUIT & VEG QUESTION

My teacher told me that I should eat five portions of fruit and veg every day . . .

. . . do strawberry laces, orange lollipops, and Jaffa Cakes count?.

4. THE SNAIL QUESTION

Is what Douglas said in the playground true? . . .

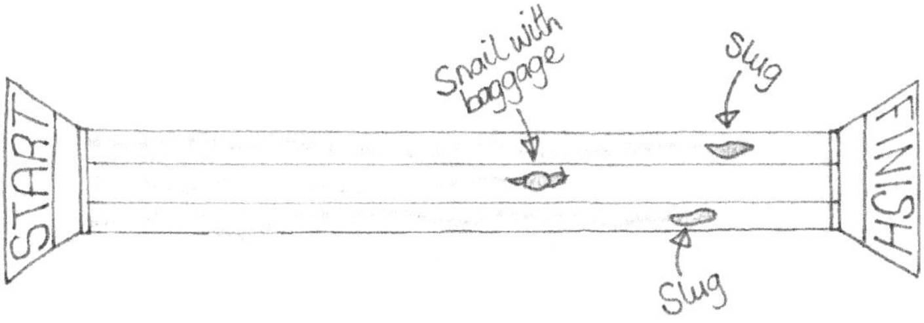
START
Snail with baggage
Slug
Slug
FINISH

. . . he said that snails are actually slugs with baggage. That's why they go slightly slower in a race.

5. THE ATLAS QUESTION

Who drew the dotted lines around the countries? . . .

. . . they must have used a huge pen!

6. THE HOT DRINKS QUESTION

Why do adults drink so much tea & coffee? . . .

. . . does it make you more intelligent? Is it a cure for some horrible terminal illness called 'aging'? It's peer pressure from your work colleagues, isn't it?

7. THE P.U. QUESTION

What does P.U. stand for, as in when someone says 'P.U. that stinks!' . . .

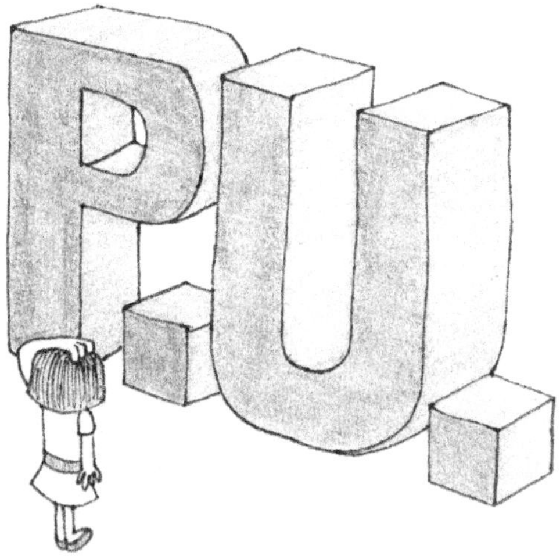
P.U.

. . . I have a few suggestions: Public Urinal, Prehistoric Underarms, Professional Uranus-ologist, Purple Umbrella.

8. THE GOD QUESTION

Can God tie a knot that he can't undo? . . .

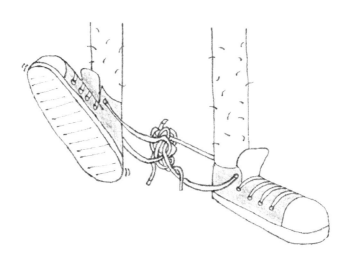

. . . because if so I'll stop praying for help untying my shoelaces and grab the scissors.

9. THE SIGN MAKER QUESTION

If sign makers were to go on strike and protest up and down the street . . .

. . . would they have to carry blank boards and empty placards?

10. THE BABIES QUESTION

I know all about where babies come from, daddies put them in mummies tummies. But I still have some extra questions . . .

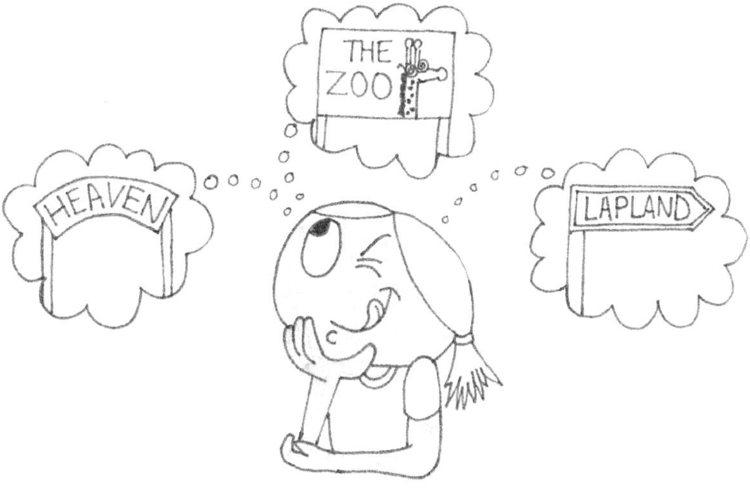
THE ZOO
HEAVEN
LAPLAND

. . . where were they before that? Do they live in heaven? Or the zoo? Or maybe Lapland? How do they get here? Who looks after them all?

James Warwood

11. THE UNDERWATER QUESTION

Can you cry underwater? . . .

. . . also can you juggle, knit, play the trumpet, or do a crossword underwater?

12. THE BAKED BEAN QUESTION

How does this tiny little baked bean turn into a loud . . .

. . . you know . . . rude, but funny noise?

13. THE PARKING QUESTION

Why do adults complain about parking so much? . . .

. . . I'm thinking of starting a business called 'The Easy Parking Rental Company'. As you're my parents you can rent any of my easy parking vehicles for half price.

14. THE PIZZA QUESTION

Would someone please explain to me why takeaway pizza comes in a square box?!? . . .

WASTED SPACE
WASTED SPACE
SPACE FOR DIP
WASTED SPACE

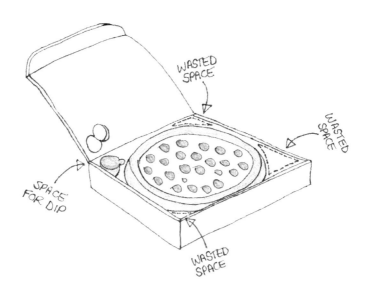

15. THE SPACE QUESTION

If I was able to persuade the worlds space agencies to join together . . .

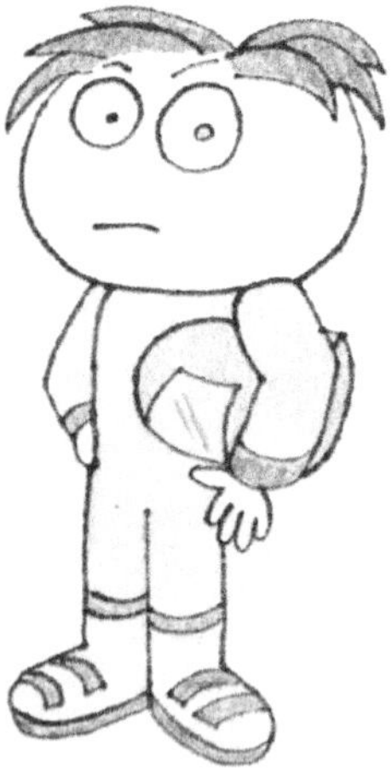

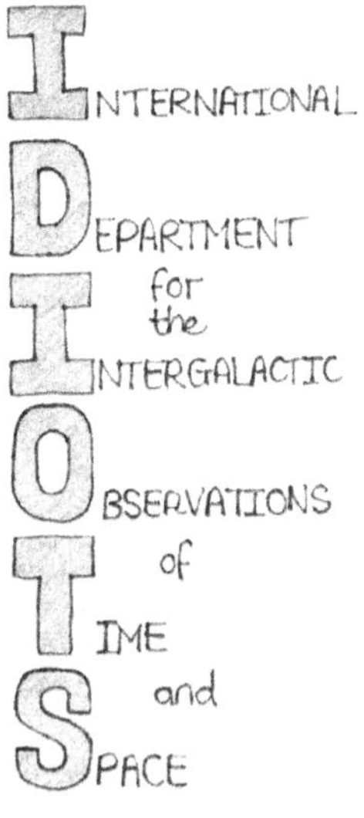
INTERNATIONAL
DEPARTMENT
for
the
INTERGALACTIC
OBSERVATIONS
of
TIME
and
SPACE

. . . could I call them I.D.I.O.T.S.

16. THE NATIONALITY QUESTION

If people who are born in America are called Americans, and people who born in Britain are called British . . .

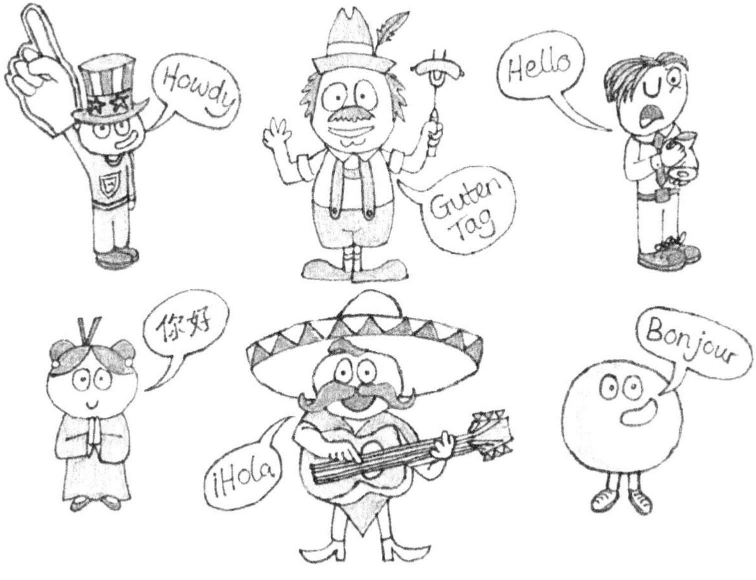
Howdy
Guten Tag
Hello
你好
¡Hola
Bonjour

. . . are people who are born in Malta called Malteasers?

17. THE GREAT FLOOD QUESTION

Were you friends with Noah or did you somehow survive the Great Flood? . . .

INVENTED BY MR WILLIAMS TO KEEP SINNERS AFLOAT.

. . . or perhaps you invented the Life Jacket!

18. THE TOOTH QUESTION

What does the Tooth Fairy do with all the teeth she collects? . . .

. . . I have a couple of working theories but would welcome the input of an adult.

19. THE CATERPILLAR QUESTION

Do butterflies remember life as a caterpillar? . . .

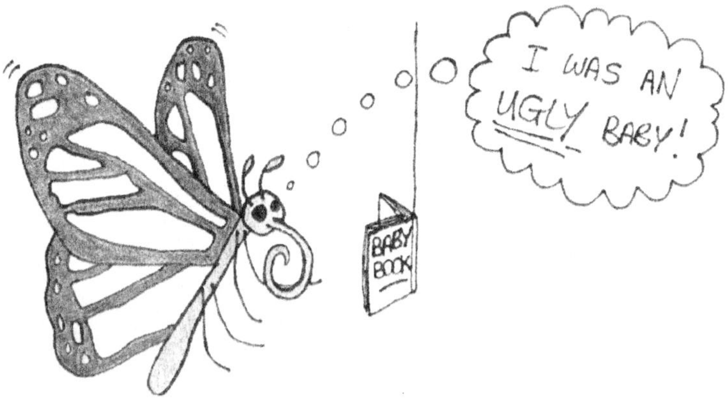
I WAS AN UGLY BABY!
BABY BOOK

20. THE CAR QUESTION

Instead of the classic car question - *'are we there yet?'* - try using SatNav lingo instead . . .

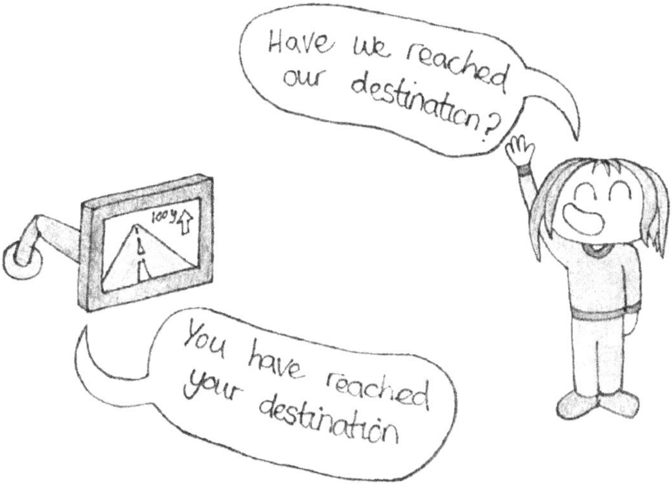
Have we reached our destination?
You have reached your destination

21. THE SPELLING QUESTION

Why do some words have a silent 'K'? . . .

. . . knock, knickers, knapsack, knob, know, knee, knowledge, knuckles . . . There is no need! If you don't give me a valid reason by the weekend I will write an angry letter to the guy who wrote the dictionary.

22. THE EVOLUTION QUESTION

If man evolved from monkeys, then how come there are still loads of monkeys? . . .

. . . are they the slow learners? The ones that didn't pass the evolution exam? Maybe they just prefer eating bananas to solving algebra?

23. THE ARK QUESTION

You know how in the Bible a man called Noah collected two of every animal, packed them on a huge boat and survived the Great Flood lasting forty days and forty nights . . .

. . . what did he do with the two woodpeckers? The only plausible explanation I can think of is that Noah invented the cork stopper.

24. THE RULE QUESTION

You know how there is an exception to every rule . . .

. . . is there an exception to that rule? Which would then mean that there is an exception to every rule apart from this one because the exception to this rule is that there is no exception negating the original exception... confused? Yeah, me too.

25. THE CHOCOLATE QUESTION

Why is chocolate not considered to be a vegetable? . . .

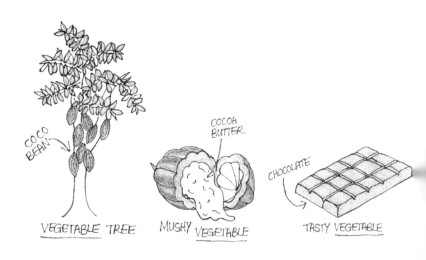

COCO BEAN
VEGETABLE TREE
COCOA BUTTER
MUSHY VEGETABLE
CHOCOLATE
TASTY VEGETABLE

. . . chocolate is made from cocoa butter . . . which is found inside cocoa beans . . . which originate from the bean family . . . which is a vegetable. Therefore chocolate should be a vegetable.

26. THE SCIENCE QUESTION

Please explain how the Hydron Collider discovered the Higgs Boson Particle.* **

* ask this question then sit back and watch your parent let out a nervous giggle, turn red in the face, then flee to the nearest broom cupboard.

** this will only work if your parent is not called Dr Higgs Boson.

27. THE CHICKEN & EGG QUESTION

Which came first, the chicken or the egg? . . .

. . . or perhaps some kind of chicken & egg mutant.

28. THE MEANING OF LIFE QUESTION

Why is the meaning of life so hard to discover? . . .

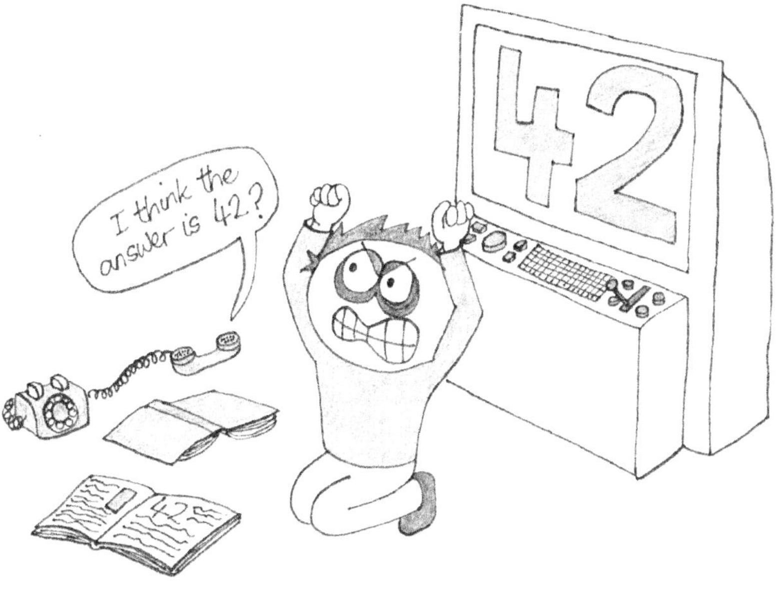
I think the answer is 42?
42
42

. . . I've got a dictionary, encyclopedia, Stephen Hawking on speed dial and a supercomputer but for some reason the only answer I ever get is the number 42!?

29. THE GAMES CONSOLE QUESTION

If God climbed down from his cloud and walked among us . . .

. . . would he buy a Playstation or an Xbox?

30. THE BEES QUESTION

Do bees have knees? . . .

. . . also, do badgers carry daggers and do weasels drink diesel?

31. THE WAVE QUESTION

Who invented waving? . . .

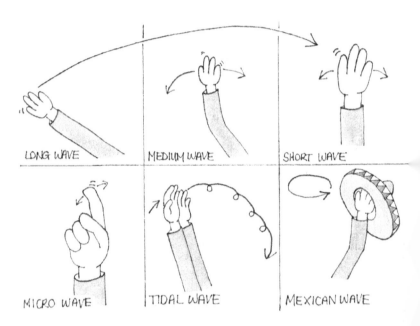

LONG WAVE

MEDIUM WAVE

SHORT WAVE

MICRO WAVE

TIDAL WAVE

MEXICAN WAVE

. . . once you find their contact details please let me know as I've got some fresh ideas they'd be interested in.

32. THE NIPPLES QUESTION

Why . . . oh why . . .

. . . do men have nipples?

33. THE PHILOSOPHICAL QUESTION

The classic philosophical question - *if a tree falls in a forest and no one is around to hear it, does it make a sound?* - that's so last century. So I've modernized it . . .

ALTERNATE REALITY

THE REAL WORLD

. . . if someone takes a selfie and shares it on Facebook but no one checks their timeline, does that person exist outside of our reality?

34. THE COUNSELLING QUESTION

Counselling for addicts is a great idea . . .

COUNSELLING IN SESSION

FOR PEOPLE ADDICTED TO COUNSELLING

. . . but what if the person becomes addicted to counselling?

35. THE SCREEN QUESTION

If staring at a screen for too long will turn your eyes square, does it work for other objects as well? . . .

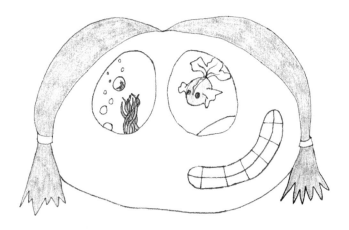

. . . if so, I am going to start staring at the fish bowl so that my pupils become little goldfish swimming around my eyeballs.

36. THE WANDERING 'W' QUESTION

Why is there no 'w' in the word 'one', but there is a silent 'w' in the word 'two'? . . .

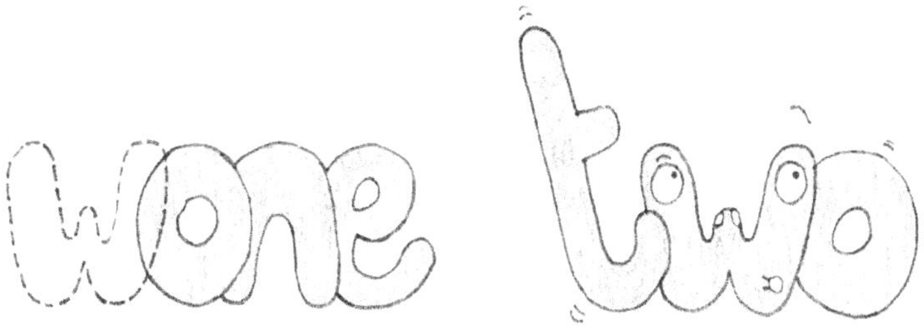
wone two

. . . somebody needs to help that 'w' find its way home.

37. THE BUTTER QUESTION

Why does a piece of buttered toast always land butter side down? . . .

. . . I think it's time we found out whether butter is the culprit once and for all!

38. THE HEAVEN QUESTION

Once you have gone to heaven, are you stuck wearing the same clothes for all eternity? . . .

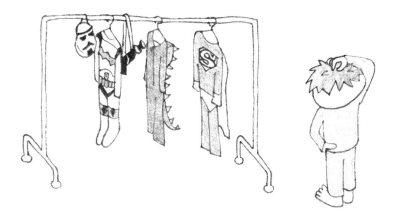

. . . if so I'm only wearing my best superhero costumes to bed from now on, just in case.

39. THE TATTOO QUESTION

Our family trip to the beach has got me thinking . . .

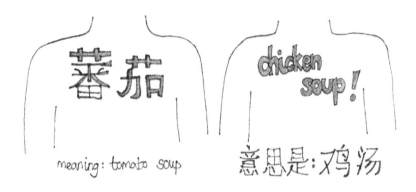

meaning: tomato soup

. . . do Chinese people get English words tattooed on their bodies?

40. THE ATHEIST QUESTION

You know how Atheists do not believe in a God . . .

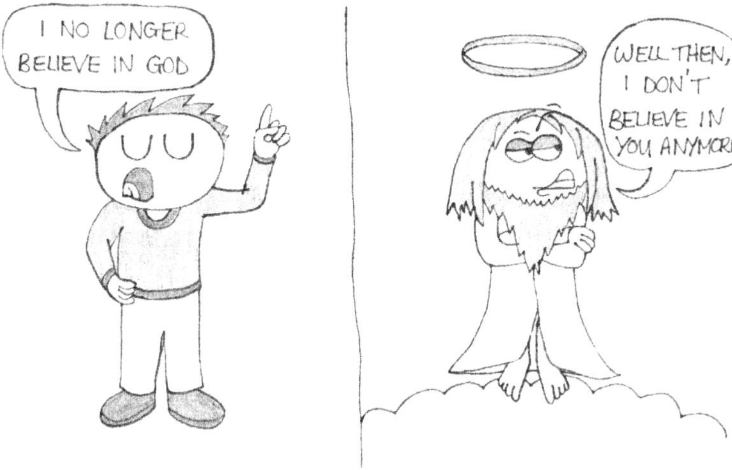
I NO LONGER BELIEVE IN GOD
WELL THEN, I DON'T BELIEVE IN YOU ANYMORE

. . . do you think that God does not believe in them either?

41. THE SPEED OF SMELL QUESTION

So we know the speed of light and we know the speed of sound . . .

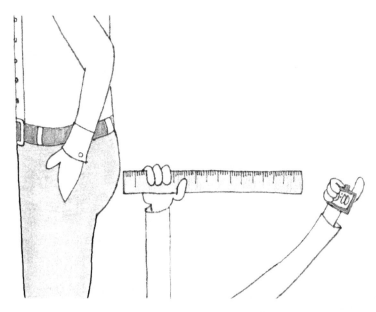

. . . but has anyone bothered to discover the speed of smell? Also could I borrow a peg please?

42. THE JOGGING QUESTION

I've been thinking, if exercise is so good for you then why do you never see a jogger smiling? . . .

. . . the people who eat chocolate, now they're the ones who look the happiest!

43. THE CRUMPET QUESTION

How do crumpets get their little holes? . . .

. . . I have some theories of my own I'd like to run them by an adult.

44. THE MARRIAGE QUESTION

You know Uncle Jim and Auntie Becca, how they say they've been together forever . . .

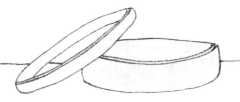

. . . does that mean that married people live longer than single people, or does it just seem longer?

45. THE PYJAMA QUESTION

If dressing gowns and pyjamas are so comfy why does everyone get dressed into boring clothes every single morning? . . .

. . . we should boycott smart shirts and long skirts and beige trousers. Join the Pyjama Revolution and never be uncomfortable ever again!

46. THE ONION QUESTION

Why is it that every time you chop an onion you cry uncontrollably? . . .

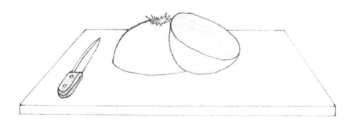

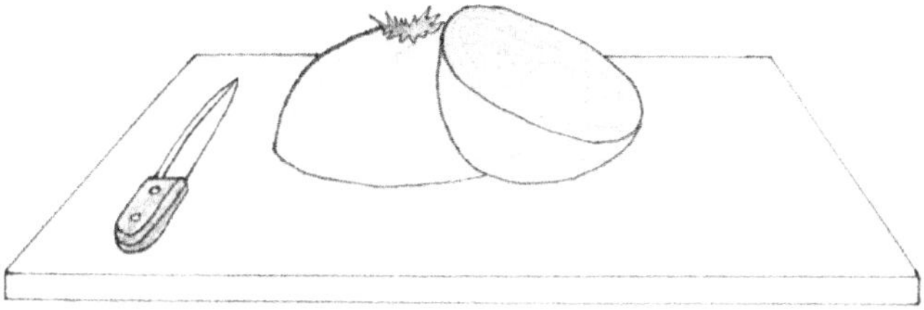

. . . did you have a traumatic childhood experience involving root vegetables? Did an onion try to kill you? There, there, I am here now, I won't let the mean onion hurt you.

47. THE CANNIBAL QUESTION

Is it true that cannibals don't eat the following people:

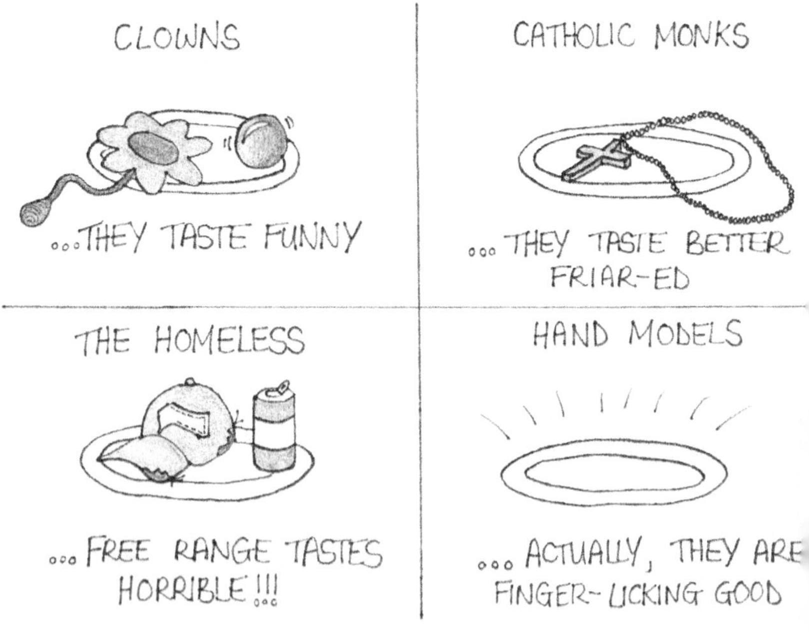

CLOWNS	CATHOLIC MONKS

...THEY TASTE FUNNY	...THEY TASTE BETTER FRIAR-ED
THE HOMELESS	HAND MODELS
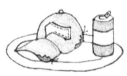	
...FREE RANGE TASTES HORRIBLE!!!	...ACTUALLY, THEY ARE FINGER-LICKING GOOD

48. THE TONGUE-TWISTER QUESTION

If Peter Piper *really* did pick a pair of pickled peppers then . . .

. . . that would make him a lying, cheating thief! Peppers don't grow in pairs. The tongue twister should be *'Sneaky Steve stole a single salted sultana'.*

49. THE HYPOTHETICAL QUESTION

Have you ever imagined a world without hypothetical situations? . . .

. . . nope, me neither.

BONUS: AMERICAN FOOTBALL QUESTION

Dear Americans . . .

. . . Why do you call it 'football' when you use your hands instead of your feet (I think)?

BONUS: DICTIONARY QUESTION

Hello, I have a question . . .

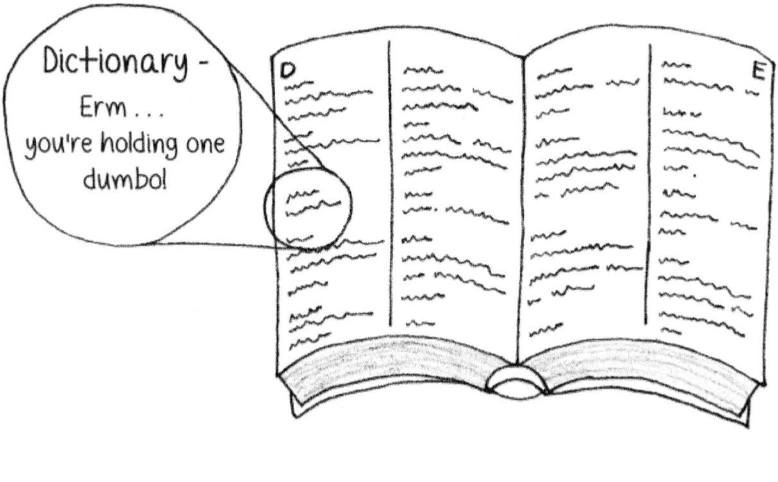
Dictionary -
Erm . . .
you're holding one
dumbo!
D
E

. . . Is the word 'dictionary' in the dictionary?

BONUS: FEATHER QUESTION

Humans find feathers extremely ticklish . . .

. . . Do birds find feathers ticklish too?

BONUS: SLICED BREAD QUESTION

So . . .

Iced Bread

Diced Bread

Spliced Bread

. . . what was the best thing *before* sliced bread?

BONUS: NATURAL BEAUTY QUESTION

Does spending three hours getting ready in the morning . . .

. . . help bring out your natural beauty?

BONUS: NEW LIFE PHILOSOPHY QUESTION

Can I adopt this modern day life philosophy? . . .

. . . 'if at first you don't succeed, complain about it on social media'.

BONUS: LOTTERY TICKET QUESTION

There, there, don't cry . . .

. . . my mother says that there are plenty of other people who don't win the lottery the first one thousand times too.

BONUS: STRANGE ADULT QUESTION

Wow! You are surprisingly polite and well-educated for an adult . . .

. . . Are you the exception to the rule or some kind of freak science fair accident?

BONUS: CATS QUESTION

Don't cry . . .

x 23

. . . one day you're going to make one (or twenty-three) cats very happy.

James Warwood

BONUS: BEAR ARMS QUESTION

Why do Americans care so much about the right to bear arms? . . .

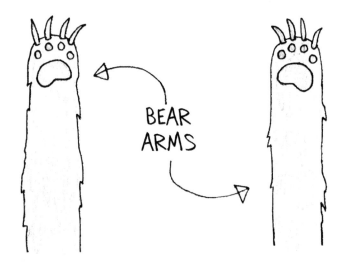

BEAR ARMS

. . . (please spare a thought for all those poor armless American bears).

BONUS: EMBARRASSING STORY QUESTION

What was your most embarrassing moment? . . .

. . . Please, just ignore all the recording devices. And I promise to never use this as blackmail.

James Warwood

BONUS: MATHS QUESTION

Why do kids have to learn how to do maths in school . . .

SMARTPHONE
(but also a calculator)

. . . when every single adult on the planet, if asked to do simple maths, just uses the calculator on their smartphone?

ABOUT THE AUTHOR

James Warwood is (usually) very good at writing about himself. So he would like to start by saying that this bio was written on an off day.

He lives on the Welsh Border with his wife, two boys, and carnivorous plant. For some unknown reason he chose a career in Customer Service, mainly because it was indoor work and involves no manual labour. He writes and illustrates children's books by night like a superhero.

Anyway, people don't really read these bios, do they? They want to get on with reading a brand new book or play outside, not wade through paragraphs of text that attempts to make the author sound like a really interesting and accomplished person. Erm . . . drat, I've lost my rhythm.

WHERE TO FIND JAMES ONLINE

Website: www.cjwarwood.com
Goodreads: James Warwood
Instagram: CJWarwood
Twitter: @cjwarwood
Facebook: James Warwood

SO, WHAT'S NEXT?

CATASTROPHE
ONE MILLION SOCKS
VANQUISHED
DRAGON

MIDDLE-GRADE STAND-ALONE FICTION

The Chef Who Cooked Up a Catastrophe
The Boy Who Stole One Million Socks
The Girl Who Vanquished the Dragon

TRUTH or POOP?
TRUTH or POOP?
TRUTH or POOP?

TRUTH OR POOP?

True or false quiz books. Learn something new and laugh as you do it!

Book One: Amazing Animal Facts
Book Two: Spectacular Space Facts
Book Three: Gloriously Gross Facts

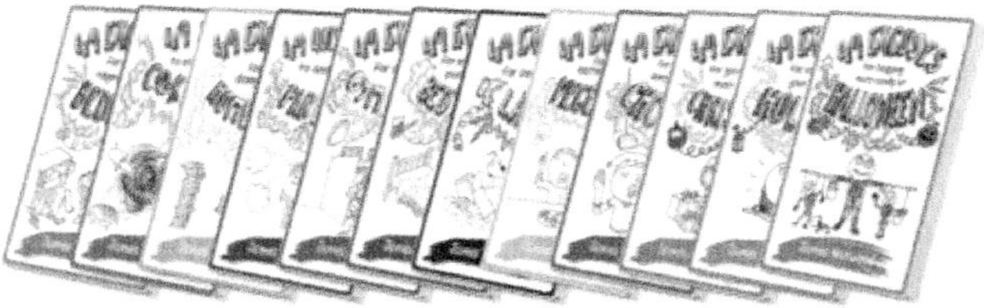

THE EXCUSE ENCYCLOPEDIA

Eleven more books to read!

Book 1 - 49 Excuses for Not Tidying Your Bedroom
Book 2 - 49 Ways to Steal the Cookie Jar
Book 3 - 49 Excuses for Not Doing Your Homework
Book 4 - 49 Questions to Annoy Your Parents
Book 5 - 49 Excuses for Skipping Gym Class
Book 6 - 49 Excuses for Staying Up Past Your Bedtime
Book 7 - 49 Excuses for Being Really Late
Book 8 - 49 Excuses For Not Eating Your Vegetables
Book 9 - 49 Excuses for Not Doing Your Chores
Book 10 - 49 Excuses for Getting the Most Out of Christmas
Book 11 - 49 Excuses for Extending Your Summer Holidays
Book 12 - 49 Excuses for Baggin More Candy at Halloween

Or get all 12 titles in 1 MASSIVE book!

The Excuse Encyclopedia: Books 1 - 12

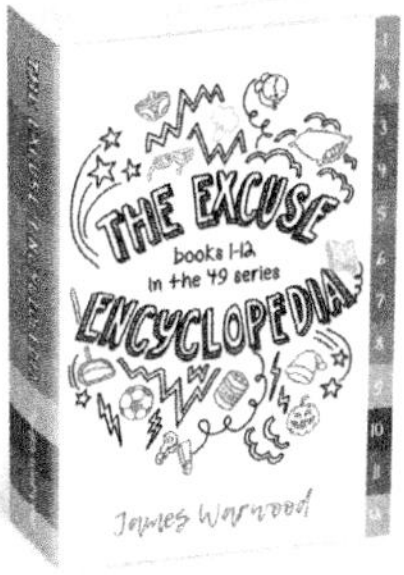
THE EXCUSE
books 1-12
in the 49 series
ENCYCLOPEDIA
James Warwood

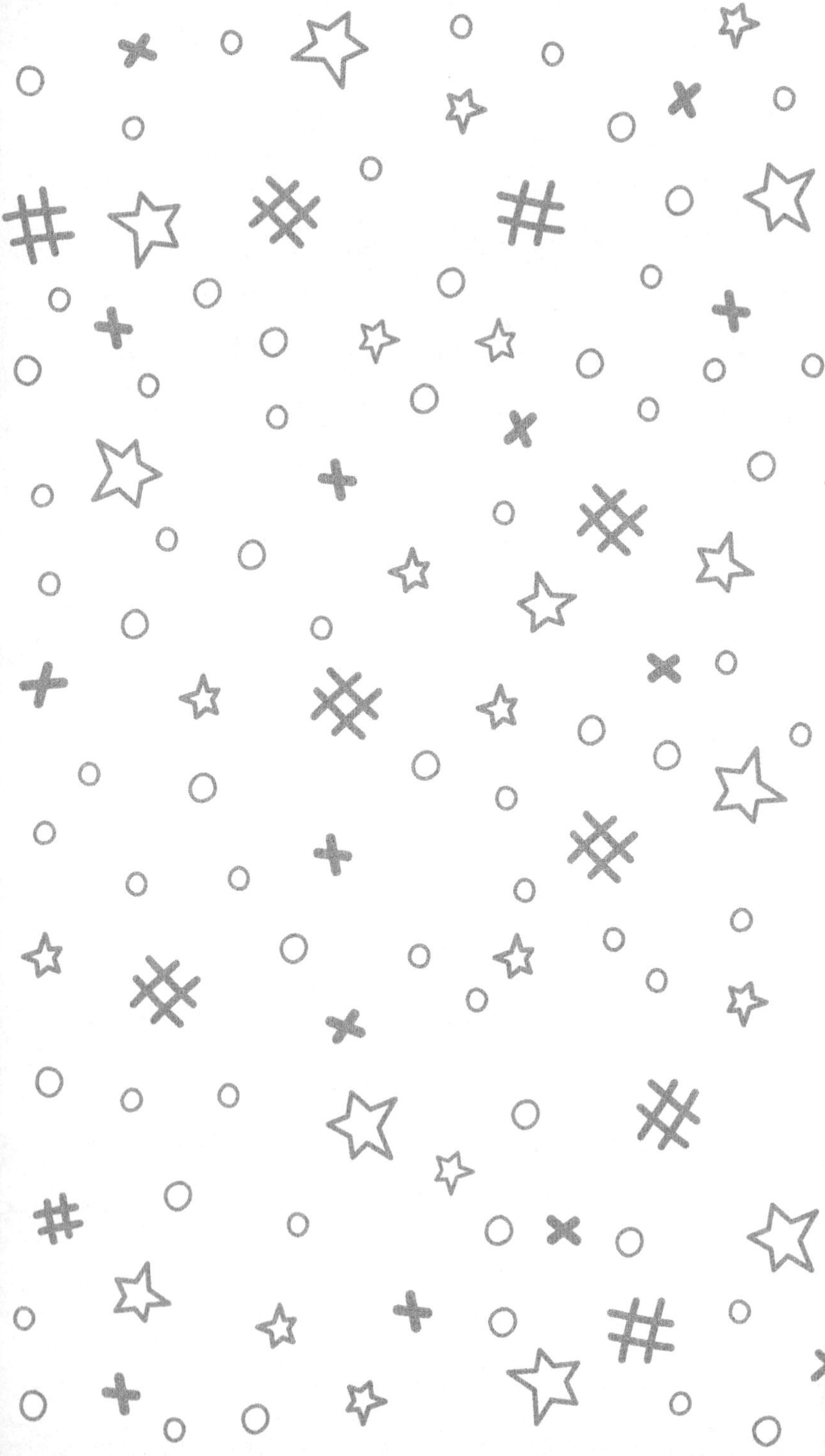

Printed in Great Britain
by Amazon